Plotlands of Shepperton

1920 - 1947

Photographs 2004 - 2016

ISBN 978-1-870736-24-4

Foreword by Judith Tucker

Plotlands of Shepperton is both delightful and disquieting in the best possible way. An important photographic enquiry into almost forgotten Thames-side, ad-hoc, plotland architecture. The evocative photographs of chalets together with the accompanying commentary gently reveal histories of ordinary people.

Szczelkun captures the make-do-and-mend aesthetic, the way the original plotlanders would work with what was to hand and through this he emphasises the communal approach in these communities. It is fascinating to see these traces of working-class culture stubbornly remaining amongst contemporary affluent suburbia. What is especially powerful is the realisation that these quirky bungalows are not so far away from the bastions of traditional power such as Eton.

The images are contrasted with apposite quotations which contextualise what we are looking at, and suddenly the photographs seem haunted, disrupted through the words, what appears to be an idyllic river scene becomes imbued with class politics, reminding us just how entwined landscape, architecture and power are. A timely work reminding us to listen to all our many histories.

Judith Tucker is an artist and winner of the Jackson's Painting category prize 2020 scenes of everyday life.

Introduction by Chris Saunders

In 'Plotlands of Shepperton' the author's gentle brilliance as a social activist brings our attention to the need to remember our strength in demanding what appears to be 'the impossible' to the neurotic neo-liberal mind. The book is an excellent historical and living (still) example of giving expression to that deep psycho-social impulse in us all to build and shape our homes and lives – that is to represent the self – to be self-determining.

Through an engaging local, personal and de-colonised social history Stefan contextualises the overlooked beauty of these waterside vernacular self-buildings that speaks in a tone that is quietly fearless and wary of the intrusions of a middle class/ruling class managers of a dominating culture of individualism that insists on a numbing conformity to its bland financialised imagination.

Stefan reminds us that by taking action collectively we are stronger and is essential to supporting our becoming more authentic individuals with our own benign agency. This book challenges the twisted common sense that we are in an individual fight against others if we want to have a better life. It reminds us that being in the mainstream doesn't have to cost you your soul.

Chris Saunders is an artist whose video works are represented by LUX, London.

Introduction

From 1959 my family lived in Manygate Lane, a road in Shepperton that goes down to the river Thames. At the time I had no consciousness about the significance of the riverside wooden chalets. I left home in 1966 to study architecture in Portsmouth, but it was not until I was on tour with the Scratch Orchestra in the North East around 1972 that I first came across a plotland community and realised that this was the architectural equivalent of improvised music. Since then I've been obsessed.

My dad Walerian sadly died in 1977. Later my mum got together with Ronald Colnbrook and finally they got married and moved into Ron's house in Thamesfield Court. This road also ends near the river, close to the Sandhills Meadow plotlands. Around 2004 I was keen to take some colour photographs with my first digital camera. I knew about a colourful set of plotland buildings on an island hidden behind Shepperton Lock. You could catch glimpses of them from the Weybridge side of the river. Hamhaugh Island was intensely private with no road access. My stepdad Ron Colnbrook agreed to come with me, as he knew someone who knew someone there and we could have the excuse of visiting them. Plotlanders were at the mercy of the planning authorities after the 1947 Town and Country Planning act, so many of the inhabitants were wary of strangers with a camera - who they might have suspected of being property developers or council officials.

Incidently, soon after this Ron was inspired to write his autobiography. He worked on it in the public library on Shepperton High Street as he didn't have a computer. 'Thursday's Child' was self-published in 2013. His life went from being a navigator in a Lancaster bomber in the war to having a steady job working for BOAC as a cargo controller. He was based all over the world, but Cairo was a BOAC hub, and that's where he met his first wife. Ron died in 2015, he was 91.

In an effort to give voice to my intuition that the plotlands are a crucial but now hidden expression of working class culture I re-read Peter Worsley's 'The Trumpet Shall Sound' (1968), which is a history of cultural resistance to imperialism at about the same period as the plotlands were forming, but on the other side of the globe. This inspired some of my footnotes.

Old Shepperton

Towpath

Pharuahs Island

Hamhaugh Island

The Lock

River Way

Cecil Ho

Why Plotlands are important to the story of working class housing since c1920.

Although there was a book-length study of the UK plotlands by Colin Ward and Dennis Hardy, published in 1984, there has since been no in-depth photographic documentation published on this wide ranging and radical solution to the nation's perennial 'housing problems'. As a student of architecture at Portsmouth in the Sixties it had struck me that common people had made their own housing for generations. In architecture this tradition is called vernacular housing. It is revered for its use of local materials which, as the geology of the UK is so varied, had resulted in a wide variety of styles. What was excised from the story of the 'vernacular' was the social history. People made these houses for themselves using local materials, skills and labour in response to need. The types of dwelling that were created can be seen in their original form at the Weald and Downland Open Air Museum. People have the capacity to do the same today.

It was only in the C19th that the wonders of municipalisation created a mind-set of housing 'provision' in the minds of the urban working class. This dependent mentality was not total and some urban folks managed to use the railways to get out and find new ways to house themselves on cheap land by rivers or by the sea-side. These people started small with a 'flat-pack' chalet, old railway carriage or a showman's wagon that had seen better days. They then built on extra rooms as needed and as finances allowed. Much if not all the work was done by family and friends. This process of gradual improvement and extension in stages gave rise to a complex aesthetic.

Of course the surviving plotlands have often been overtaken by rising property prices and are no longer homes for the poor. Some have been replaced by bland brick boxes others have become 'grand designs'. The closer shots in the collection that follows are chosen of houses where the original plotland house form is still evident. The more distant shots across the Thames will show the actual variety of housing. Some planning authorities now have quietly enlightened approaches to retaining some of the character of the original. Spelthorne Council that presides over the Shepperton area has been one such.

The 'footnotes' that run along the bottom of the following pages are numbered but the numbers are just to separate and identify each note and do not always refer to the picture above. They are a river of words which are intended to reflect deeper significance into the images floating above them. Notes followed by small page numbers are quotes from Dennis Hardy & Colin Ward 1984.

Hamhaugh Island 2004

A few years earlier I'd bought my first video camera - the Sony PD100. It was a 'three chip' camera so the colour was good and it also did stills with sound. As I said, my step-dad Ronald 'knew someone' but it still felt a bit like we were snoopers and might be called out for 'trespassing'. As a child explorer of Shepperton I would often come across signs saying, 'NO TRESPASSERS' and wonder if I should fear them.

Hamhaugh Island - the story as told by Valerie Brooking (1995)

"My mother's family camped at Hamhaugh during August, after the hay was mown, from 1900. On the first occasion they came in a horse-drawn van containing tents, bedding, stove, provisions etc, from Chelsea." At this time camping was not considered to be respectable.

1914 wooden floors and camp beds had replaced tarpaulins and bed rolls. In 1918 someone records using a folding wood and canvas bath. Sheds were erected and used as kitchens. Until 1919 there were communal latrines. Then the landowner Jack Dunton decided to sell plots to the campers...

c1920 the first 'bungalow' or shack was erected.

1928 - The first family stayed all year around. From 1926 to 1939 there was a golden age of community activity, with regattas and fancy dress dances on the green. Later the green was bought collectively to keep it as a common open space.

1938 - The last use of seasonal tents - the shanty community was now complete.

1940s - A communal water pump was sunk on the green.

1948 - The arrival of electricity replaced oil lamps. The majority of houses now became permanent homes.

1959 - Mains water arrived to three stand pipes on the Green.

"During the next twenty years bungalows became larger and more elaborate, usually by successive additions to the original shack." Winifred Scholfield. p11.

"Yes it's a shack on an island... no, it's a small island, in fact the shack is a bit small too... Some people call them bungalows but shack is the word for this... its made of wood, yes wood." Daphne Silver. p33.

"Those who purchased plots gave them bizarre names – Whyworrie – Weyknot – Watabatit. There was a toilet in the middle of the green. A flag was hoisted when it was in use!" Joy Noble. p28.

'Shepperton's Island Dwellers'

Valerie Brooking, 1995.

Hamhough Island 2004

THE OUTPOST, CYGNETS, **STADBURY**, SANS SOUCI, **HIGH TREES**, Idle Waters, FAIRWAY, BRAMERTON, WEYBAK, NUTSHELL, the river house, LAZYLANDS, **THAMES HOUSE**, SPUR COTTAGE, Twenty One, **WITT'S END**, SINA, WILD THYME, **THE HAVEN**, BELLE-VUE, By The Wey, WEIR SOUND, **JOYLANDS**, GREENSIDE.

Taking new names to symbolise a new life. See Peter Worsley, The Trumpet Shall Sound, p

Many of the 1920s plotland pioneers must have carried trauma from WW1. If not from having survived combat, then because of losing close family members or friends. These environments must have had a soothing effect on such troubled souls. On top of this there was a shortage of housing and those returning from the war **were of a mind to take matters into their own hands.** (See p.17 Hardy & Ward)

Fading memories of community games on Hamhough Island in 2003

1. Going back to the early days in the 1920s when the pioneering spirit of the original plot-holders was strong we imagine that the community included early bohemian movie-makers and silent film stars. Shepperton Studios was only started in 1930 but Cecil Hepworth had started a studio in Walton in 1899, which was walking distance from Hamhaugh Island. 2. River dreaming was part of the lure of the Thameside shanties. The sound of the mighty river, punctuated by the calls of marine birds, can evoke a soporific mood. Some magical mornings the undulating back of the river is reflected onto the ceiling over the bed. In late afternoons a river light can flood the room.

Walking from Desborough Cut to Walton Bridge in September 2012.

'Since 1900 improved road and rail links with London and a growing appreciation of countryside values stimulated e demand for housing on the Thames riverbank between Thames Ditton and Staines-upon-Thames. Two background tors produced a supply of riparian building land, sold-on in small parcels, to create a 'plotland' landscape: firstly, the eak-up of landed estates following a doubling of death duties and the slaughter of male heirs during World War I and, condly, in the interwar years, the supply of cheap farmland from bankrupt owners hit by the economic recession.'
bury Matters magazine, 2018

4. 'The gravel from the excavation [of Desborough Cut between 1930 and 1935,] was piled on the opposite bank, and the settlement there began with a former showman's caravan belonging to an insurance clerk. It evolved into a string riverside plots with a 40-foot frontage, between the meadow and the river, with to the north, a similar curve of riverside plots known as Sandhills Meadow.' p.178 **5.** Some of the first shelters were old single-decker Midland buses. the1980s there was: "A close-knit community of residents who are all old friends." p.179

In 1950 Eric de Maré, the leading architectural photographer, thought the dwellings were: "far more pleasing than
suburbia proper, partly because water, with its moving reflections, mitigates all ugliness and partly because many of
these bungalows have a certain homemade charm... We should not scorn these amateur pieces of architecture for
they are a kind of modern folk art, the crude and unselfconscious origins of a culture which limited spare time has
nurtured, and which only more and more spare time together with greater affluence can encourage and develop."

7. 'The very disorder and freedom which newcomers brought was anathema to the self-appointed guardians of a more traditional landscape.' p.34 **8.** Clough Williams Ellis was one of these who saw the plotlanders 'destroying and dishonouring it with shoddy but all-to-permanent encampments'. 1951. Ellis was one of the middle class voices who campaigned for the 1947 Town and Country Planning Act, which was to effectively put an end to any further such incursions by the poor. But the existing plot-holders put up an effective legal and political defence of their holdings and resisted all the efforts of the local authorities to remove them.

To the left just outside the frame of this photograph is Walton Bridge. The new bridge was being built when I took these photographs in 2012. **10.** Further upstream the river Thames has Eton, Windsor and Henley on its banks. No wonder then that the plotlands of the Thames Valley attracted the full weight of establishment disapproval. It must have seemed like an invasion of a sanctuary of the privileged class. **11.** The dominant class have 'an obsessive fear of number, of undifferentiated hordes indifferent to (class) difference and constantly threatening to submerge the private spaces of bourgeois exclusiveness.' p.469 Pierre Bourdieu 1979.

Views along Thames Meadow

12. As the construction of the first huts and shelters was underway there was a conviviality and a sharing of tools and and building materials like roofing felt and nails. This forged a sense of community amongst neighbours relatively unknown in the conventional more individualistic suburban houses to the north. **13.** The plotlands were the fulfilment of a long-standing current of English revolt in relation to land-rights, from the The Diggers on nearby St George's Hill, Weybridge in 1649 to the Chartist Land Plan of the 1840s.

4. The common starter structure was a chalet with two room and a veranda. The 1910 trade catalogue of W. Gardam Sons (who were located just upstream at Staines Bridge Wharf): "In placing before your notice the following designs for WEEK-END, SEA-SIDE and UP-RIVER BUNGALOWS we would call attention to the fact that we are prepared to ERECT, FIT and DECORATE same in any part of the UNITED KINGDOM, complete and ready for occupation at COMPETITIVE PRICES" These would have been brought down river on a barge from Staines. Current price for a similar insulated timber structure starts at about £6000.

15. This modernised chalet has used an unusual variant of the A-Frame to provide a second floor within the roof. This was a solution to the needs for more space that was also found acceptable to the planning department by the architec Owen Short in his work on the chalet fields of the Gower. (See the companion volume). **16.** At the time the plotlands were taking off, the air in polluted cities like London was so poor it was the cause of respiratory illnesses and premature death. Seeking fresh air in plotland locations was a sensible move and probably a life saver for many.

. Indeed, the whole aesthetic of the plotlands might be considered as an unleashing of taste that flew in the face of e establishment. "In all respects, plotlands stood out as the very antithesis of the normal, old-fashioned village England d the values that it represented. Plotland complexes were ephemeral, unsightly, anarchistic and an affront to good te; in complete contrast, the long-established English village, was seen by middle-class observers as the acceptable it of countryside living." (Rowley, 2006, p. 211)

18. These were the first people I spoke to. Plotlanders are often suspicious of intruders pointing cameras, but these people were very friendly and invited me in to look around. The second photograph was taken in their riverside garde
19. Plotlands were an idealistic drop-out movement flying in the face of the banality of a 'mortgage for life'. Heading o into the margins to get rid of the burden of rent and to have less dependency on a steady job. Avoiding the trap of a consumer nightmare of hire-purchase repayments and keeping up with the Jones'. Living the dream of an extended holiday by the seaside or river.

20. The natural reflex of house building by a community to provide homes for its members had been BLOCKED for the first time in human history. This was a deep unrecognised disturbance in the common psyche. **21.** 'The recollection of plotland people is a simple tale of quiet enjoyment, without personal gain or pretension. Almost without exception our interviews revealed that plotlanders themselves retain fond memories of childhood holidays and a kind of pioneering experience.' p.276

Walking downstream from Walton Bridge in March 2014.

22. We should not underestimate the powerful emotions engendered in a group by a conscious mobilisation to overthrow the established ways to provide a home for ones family, and to adopt radically new ones. (See Peter Worsley p.9)
23. 'Community' had little or no value in the capitalist scheme of things. Working class communities created over generations were not understood in the world of literary knowledge. Their value was rarely represented. To the plann or developer community was often just an impediment to business.

. A century or so ago it would have broken peoples hearts not to provide shelter for the needy in their parish. My
eat grandmother, Granny Johnson, was one such needy person in the early C20th. Her husband died when he was
st 35 years old leaving ten children with no welfare. With no income the family lost their rented house but the
mmunity gave them an earth-walled cottage in a hamlet called Little Lunnon in Lincs. There seems to have been no
eds or payments involved. It was only the most basic shelter but it allowed my family to survive.

25. 'The bungalows, by the exercise of every possible eccentricity and mark of individuality, break up the line of the ri
Each house has its gable, its weathervane, each plot its fence and railing, its flagstaff, its name-board and its crazy pavir
Planning Report 1930. **26.** WANTED! insight into the oral culture of the plotlanders. One day we may discover journ
or letters that have left a record of what people did in the first 40 or 50 years. The recent work of artists like Karen
Guthrie and Nina Pope's documentary, *Jaywick Escapes*, (2012) or Harriet Tarlo and Judith Tucker's recent project usin
paintings, poems and writing about the Humberston 'Fitties' has given us the start of such knowledges.

7. The initiative to make a home might have been driven by need but it was also a form of *cultural* expression. I would suggest that the realisation of direct, unmediated political power depends on everyday cultures to express, channel and evolve social needs. Class oppression will only be overcome when working class culture can assert and defend itself. Historically, working class cultural expression has been blocked, unfunded or made to seem insignificant by the British cultural establishment.

The Towpath at Shepperton Lock - January 2016

28. The proletarians coming out from the burgeoning towns were opposed by a broad church of middle class preservationists who mounted a romantic and conservative defence of the British landscape, along with its class structure and general way of life. This was in the context of a general distaste for *all* popular uses of the countryside.

29. 'Very few public voices were raised to suggest that the plotlander's bungalow had a place in the riverside landscape. Yet by the 1980s, when the remaining ones have merged into the landscape, with grass, trees and foliage, they have become the least obtrusive, and for many, the most interesting, of all the Thameside buildings.' P.188

. It is a universal aspect of all human societies to provide ourselves with adequate shelter - given that we have access
 space and materials. In time, if there is not absolute poverty or trauma, these will become beautiful. **31.** The surviving
otlands are striking evidence of 'how much was achieved by relatively poor people with few resources beyond their
n labour and enthusiasm.' p.294

32. Originally this chalet would have had an open veranda looking out over the river. **33.** Despite a sense of friendliness and mutual aid, despite their rapid spread across the country and despite their unique architectural style, the UK plotlands was not an integrated movement with a unitary authority structure. The reverse is the case, they were a leaderless response to their time and the opportunities that it afforded common people. **34.** Shepperton's railway station opened on 1st November 1864. The electrification of the line occurred in 1916 which increased the attraction of this destination to the early pioneers.

5. Looking across the river to Pharoahs Island which can only be accessed by boat. This can be dangerous when the river is high. The actor Ian Hendry used to live in the big house on the left of the picture. I remember him in The Avengers. 36. 'Although essentially a landscape of the poor this very fact, in turn, attracted to such areas its own bohemian clientele. Actors and actresses, artists and writers, stars of music hall and early film enjoyed and, in turn, contributed to the libertarian atmosphere of such places.' p.2

37. The plotlanders knew the attitudes of the establishment to their starter homes. The animosity of the authorities taught them lessons on security and publicity. The extent of homes was often hidden behind bushes and other lush foliage that reduced the visibility of spatial developments. This reflex to hide persists and older residents can be wary of people 'inspecting' their property. **38.** Working class culture was not considered a proper object of study, so we don't know if plotland dwellers evolved unique cultural responses to the place in which they lived. As a distinctive group they are a people outside of history.

I was an angler as a teenager and sometimes used to fish here in about 1961. I would have liked to have caught a ʳbel but in spite of reading Isaac Walton's 'The Compleat Angler', I think my best catch was a Perch. **40.** 'We wanted a ace which was primitive, where the children could do what they liked. They could play pirates, build rafts, fall in the ʳer and get covered in mud, and nobody minded.' p.170. **41.** The plotlanders were living the dream of leisure that had en dangled in front of them for centuries.

42. The plotlands were the product of the ambivalent feelings of a people torn between hatred of the middle classes, who had destroyed the old way of life and had now dominated them for a century or more with the wage system an the Metropolitan police force, and the desire to obtain for themselves some of the leisure long enjoyed by the class who lorded it over them. **43.** "In the poetics of struggle and lived experience, in the utterances of ordinary folk, in th cultural products of social movements, in the reflections of activists, we discover the many different cognitive maps o the future, of the world not yet born." Robin D. G. Kelley, 2003

4. Across the river is Pharoah's Island. Most of the fourteen dwellings on this island have Egyptian names. Apparently the island was given to Admiral Nelson after his victory in the Battle of the Nile in 1798 and was subsequently used as his 'fishing retreat'. Was this a euphemism for nookie with Lady Hamilton? **45.** The violent rivalry between English and French Imperialism led to this legendary sea battle in which Admiral Lord Nelson routed the French fleet under Napoleon Bonaparte. This lead to the birth of Egyptology and the 'Middle East' being rediscovered by European Orientalists. But the island was simply known as 'Dog Ait' until the end of the C19th.

46. I haven't chosen these dwellings for their sometimes cute or shambolic quality. It's meant to be an honest study of the plotlands warts and all, as they exist in the Shepperton area. However, I have focused on those with a recognisable connection to their beginnings. Some plotland communities are now almost indistinguishable from an estate of typical suburban chalet bungalows. **47.** The Plotlands were, 'essentially, very modest places offering simple pleasures for generally poor people.' (p.278) but this underplays the demotic unconscious that was being allowed a deep draught of freedom.

. Did plotlands contain an unseen part of a metaphysical and strategic secret? "In a globalised world, cargo cult, like ~stom, has become a metaphor for the domination of capitalism and the general homogenisation of nation state ~vernance." Marc Tabani, 2013. We should remember that there is no impermeable membrane between the mundane and ~e magical. Colin Ward and Dennis Hardy report only the mundane facts in a rather meek or officious form of ~guage. We have yet to hear the plotland *kastom* roaring like the Shepperton weirs.

Sandhills Meadow March 2013

49. So the value of plotlands is not *just* the self-provision of shelter. Nor is it *just* making a home, in a community. The are not simply a technical solution to keeping 'rain off our heads' but are also a form of working class cultural expression - an art of architectural improvisation. 50. The suburbs were part of a dream to escape the condescensio of public housing *provision* by rich philanthropists with its 'progressive' but rigid space standards, and an invitation to enjoy the legal 'rights' that came with property ownership.

1. Plotlands were like cargo cults in that they were unusual, marginal, powerful, and perceived as a dangerous phenomena that opposed the conventions of the establishment, who saw them as irrational and disorderly. **52.** Land sales were prompted by pre-war legislation. In the four years after WWI about one quarter of English land was sold. Nothing on this scale had occurred since the dissolution of the monasteries. **53.** Meanwhile out in the colonies: The best economic land had *passed out* of native possession.' A euphemism for it having been stolen by the sleight of hand by which 'land ownership' is registered as a written claim. The people forced to become indentured labourers.

54. At the end of World War II the state feared disturbances from de-mobilised soldiers, including a squatter movement after many Londoners were made homeless by the German Blitz. The plotland movement might have taken off on a larger scale occupying spaces like Royal Parks! The election of a Labour government quickly passed the 1947 Town and Country Planning Act, which curtailed any such popular initiatives, and then instituted a municipal house building programme. To make way for these highly profitable corporate housing developments, terraced housing was targeted for 'slum' clearance rather than being distributed for piecemeal renovation by urban plot holders.

. Some suburbs became crucibles of individuated dreams when the alienated reality of the loss of urban community
: home. Shepperton had different elemental forces brought into an untidy conjunction. Lord Nelson and the river,
hoes of empire in the yacht club. London Airport with its association with the Battle of Britain and some transatlantic
ure from the supersonic Concorde. The M3 Motorway sliced through with a constant rumble of lorries full of 'cargo'.
e scenario was heightened by the dumb presence of the movie industry and the stars that were drawn there; bricks
ainst shacks; dumps and gravel pits; an unholy disorder of parts; a fragmented and faded glamour.

56. "They slept, our hikers, in Danny's Plotlands chalet. Most of the original structures, built by naturists and fresh-air buffs, had disappeared under tarmac, new estates. A breath of the countryside in the Langdon Hills for those decanted from East London by war or ambition: put up whatever you fancy, a small patch of ground. Walks, grass-cutting, singsongs. By motorcycle and sidecar, or train (with a hike at the end), they came in their hundreds." Ian Sinclair, 2004

Sandhills Meadow - September 2012

7. It is often when I find these original but close to wrecked examples that I get a yearning to live in one. I see it all done up in bright colours. But even a wrecked one in this area is well beyond my means. **58.** Shepperton has a split personality - the river shanty people with their houses on stilts, a rowing boat at the ready, set against the semi-detached people who are oblivious to the reality of being surrounded by water. To the north the embankments of the seven hundred acre Queen Mary reservoir tower fourteen meters over them.

The Creek, Lower Sunbury road. May 2020

59. As I would journey to Sunbury along the Lower Sunbury road quite often in the Sixties, this 'Egyptian shanty' with its orientalist dome and minaret touches made its way into my imagination in a persistent way that is hard to rememb exactly. Looking at the photo now I've a sense of disbelief at how small the dome and spire actually are. In my memory they were huge. For me it really broke the mould of what a house should be in a radical way.

. I don't think I'd read *The Arabian Nights* but Aladdin's magic carpet and Ali Baba's forty thieves were everywhere in
ildren's books, comics, cartoons and pantomimes. One of the songs in the recent Disney version of 'Aladdin' speaks of
and 'Where it's flat and immense and the heat is intense, It's barbaric, but hey, it's home'. So unfortunately orientalism
still alive and well. Although before doing this book I had no idea it had such a part in my adolescent landscape.

Garricks Ait, Hampton, June 2013

61. Continuing downstream towards London there are more of these dwellings both on the river and clustered around the inlets of smaller streams and on islands. After Sunbury the road winds through some rather imposing water treatment works before it comes to Lower Hampton. Before reaching Tagg's Island there is a clear view across the river from the main road heading for Hampton Court.

Eel Pie Island,
Twickenham,
December 2016

2. Eel Pie Island, with its evocative edible name has played another big part of my life. The island is reached by a
•otbridge and so there are no roads on the island. The island sits facing the main river frontage of the Twickenham
•wn so is perhaps the most urban of plotland sites.

63. I once cycled over to Eel Pie from Shepperton when I was about 15 to hear The Rolling Stones play in the old hot (c1963). Later c1970 my friend Clifford Harper lived in a pretty wild commune there and I would occasionally visit. On I was sleeping in my van on the mainland when there was a police raid. Torch beams shone through the cracks in the v door - I had to keep very still and quiet. These photos were taken on a recent visit with our Museum Visiting Group to see the annual open studio event.

C19 municipalisation had *provided* us with the wonders of civil engineering (Clean water, sewage, energy etc) in exchange for a mind-set of dependency. The Local Authorities provided housing, parks, dustbin collections and local schools in exchange for our passive acceptance that the provision of these basic human needs was organised and managed by the class on high in order to make their own personal fortunes. Along with this was a passive acceptance *their* patriarchal values, *their* literary culture and *their* media representations of all that was 'news'.

For contrast this is **a 'typical' 1930s Semi-D** in Shepperton. The thing that distinguishes this particular one is that it was the home of J.G. Ballard, arguably Britain's most radical modernist writer. He lived in Shepperton from 1960 to when he died in 2009. Ballard was downwardly mobile middle-class in terms of domestic property at least. Shepperton is often referred to as a 'middle class' suburb. The very small area around Old Shepperton is certainly up-market but on the whole Shepperton is marked by a dull ordinariness.

Ballard's horrific book *'The Unlimited Dream Company'* (1979) is set in Shepperton. The psychotic anti-hero showers Shepperton with his semen and plans and commits atrocities against the inhabitants. Ballard describes the people of Shepperton by occupation. It's not so much the mythical middle class suburban village, as described in Wikipedia and the local estate agents, but more the small town of: garage mechanics, a train driver, secretaries and typists, bank clerks, dark-suited executives carrying their briefcases, receptionists, teachers, shopkeepers, newspaper delivery boys, a retired soldier with a shooting stick, amateur actors in Shakespearean costume, postmen, office cleaners, milkmen, housewives, film actors, artisans and bank cashiers, car salesmen and dubbing mixers, film technicians, a butcher, mechanics in greasy overalls, a village policeman, accountants, shoe salesmen, computer programmers and more secretaries. This list rings true to my own memory of the time that I lived there.

65. Shepperton proper, from the Church Square up to the Ballard end of the high street, is almost a flip side of the plotlands that line the river Thames. The *conventional* suburbs as against the dangerous autonomous plotlands. Both sh something of the same arcadian dream, but the semi-D's and brick bungalows, are safer (from flood and in terms of investment) than the timber plotland chalets, but they are also more timid and less adventurous.

The plotlands did aim to extend 'the holidays' into a life of common leisure. Bohemian occasionally, but more often a microcosmic creative lifestyle of macrame and evening class painters. My mum being one.

John Gregson a film star famous in the Fifties and Sixties (Inspector Gideon) lived in Creek House in Old Shepperton and went to our RC church between 1958 - 75 providing a touch of glamour to the tedious mass intoned in Latin. The film studios was always in the back of your mind living in Shepperton. 'The Guns Of Navarone' could be heard blasting away from our chalet bungalow in Manygate Lane soon after we moved in in 1960. More recently another Catholic film star, Ruth Wilson (b.1982, Alice in Luther), was a kind neighbour to my mum and Ron in their old age.

The tales of the sensational C18th courtesan and performance artist Emma Hamilton who lived, on occasion, in a house around the corner from Manygate Lane from about 1782 - 85 provides an earlier undercurrent of a distant bohemian culture. Emma later became the lover of Admiral Lord Nelson (c1793) and mother of his child, Horatia, who was born in 1801. It all adds a strange sense of second-hand glamour. A glamour that is tainted by the era and mal-eros of its roots in Empire and Orientalism.

"Nothing is ever terminal, thank God. As we hesitate, the road unrolls itself, dividing and turning. But there is something deeply suffocating about life today in the prosperous west. Bourgeoisification, the suburbanisation of the soul, proceeds at an unnerving pace. Tyranny becomes docile and subservient, and a soft totalitarianism prevails, as obsequious as a wine waiter. Nothing is allowed to distress and unsettle us. The politics of the playgroup rules us all." JG Ballard interviewed by fax by Jeannette Baxter in 2004

6. Collective building activity is one of the key differences between the riverside dwellings that started as self-built halets in the 1920s or '30s and the often lonely life in suburban brick and mortar houses on higher ground away from he River. 67. An old friend who grew up in this area messaged me: "I sometimes reflect on my post-war suburban hildhood which I had always thought was inferior to growing up in a community where everyone had shared roots." .W. June 2020.

Bibliography

Ballard, J.G. *The Drowned World*, 1962 and, *The Unlimited Dream Company*, 1979

Bourdieu, Pierre. *Distinction: A Social Critique of the Judgement of Taste.* 1979

Brooking, Valerie. *Shepperton Island Dwellers*, SSLHS, 1995

Colnbrook, Ronald. *Thursdays Child*, Shepperton, 2013

Kelley, Robin D. G. *Freedom Dreams: The Black Radical Imagination*, 2003

de Maré, Eric. *London's Riverside*, 1958

Rowley, Trevor. *The English Landscape in the Twentieth Century*, 2006

Sinclair, Ian. *Dining on Stones (or, The Middle Ground)*, 2004

Szczelkun, Stefan. *The Conspiracy of Good Taste*: (orig.1993) 2017

Tabani, Marc. *Kago, Kastom and Kalja: The Study of Indigenous Movements in Melanesia Today*, 2013

Tarlo, Harriet, and Judith Tucker. 'neverends: poems and paintings', Wild Pansy Press, 2018

Williams, Kate. *England's Mistress: The infamous life of Emma Hamilton*, 2006

Williams Ellis, Clough. *Town and Country Planning*, 1951

Worsely, Peter. *The Trumpet Shall Sound*, (orig. 1956), 1968

The Scratch Cottage 197

Companion publication

Chalet Fields of the Gower

New pocket edition - improved photographic print quality.

Short Description: Photographic documentation of two of the Chalet Fields of the Gower in South Wales, plus an interview with local architect Owen Short. The book shows the evolution of these colourful wooden houses over the last few decades in a series of over 70 beautifully reproduced colour photographs that show their distinctive attraction and value as a form of housing. This is the first book length photographic study of a UK plotlands.

70 Colour photographs, plus an interview with architect Owen Short

70 pages, 165 x 165mm, paperback, £16

NB New ISBN 978-1-870736-23-7

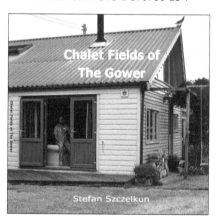

Related Titles:

The Conspiracy of Good Taste: William Morris, Cecil Sharp and Clough Williams-Ellis and the repression of working class culture in the C20th This is a new deluxe paperback edition of the 1993 original in which the history of the plotlands is explored in relation to some of the main middle class oppressors, including Clough Williams-Ellis. ISBN 978-1-870736-71-8

SILENCE! The great silencing of British working class culture since the C19th. This book continues the themes of The Conspiracy of Good Taste with new research and expanded terms of reference. It is presented in a full colour graphic format. The central argument is that there can be no ending of class oppression without a fully supported working class culture in every sense media.
ISBN 978-1-870736-22-0

SENSE THINK ACT - In this follow up to the Survival Scrapbooks study of basic life supports Szczelkun explores elemental human abilities and suggest they could be the basis of rethinking culture, religion, and educational curricula.   ISBN 978-1-870736-12-1

Also available as ebooks.

Books afford a certain autonomy and mobility that other forms of art works do not. Also, deeply embedded social patterns, like those holding class oppression in place, need to be opposed in a very persistent way if we are to change them. Books tend to stick around and stay in circulation.

There may be a final edition in this series that will be 'fifty of the best' Plotland shanty chalets in the UK to show how widespread the phenomena is. I made a group on Flickr a decade or so ago and It has a very wide ranging collection of plotland dwellings. I also have many photos of my own that have not been included in the Shepperton and Gower books.

About the author

The author went to Portsmouth to study architecture in 1966. The discomfort he felt with the profession resulted in his 'Survival Scrapbook Shelter' which was published by Unicorn Bookshop in Brighton in 1972. 'Food' and 'Energy' followed in 1974 and a Schocken Book edition of all three was published in North America. It was around this time that he first came across a colourful plotland community in Ovingham outside Newcastle, whilst touring with the Scratch Orchestra. The buildings seemed to be a form of architectural improvisation akin to the free-form collective music making he was experiencing. Later he set up a building project for the musicians and this was shown as 'The Scratch Cottage' in the 'Art Spectrum' exhibition in 1971.

It was later in 1983 whilst teaching in Hull that he met architect Phil Wren whose thesis showed him how the Plotlands were an integral part of the pursuit of leisure by the working class. By now the plotlands had become a core interest in his wider study of working class culture. In spite of Hardy and Ward's publication of 'Arcadia for All' in 1984 there has been little in the way of photographic documentation published. A rare example was 'Severn Heaven' a video made by Jonathan Meades which was first broadcast in 1990.

It was in the early 1990s after fifteen years of squatting that he had the good fortune to become a member of Sharsted Street Self-Build Co-op in Kennington. In three years from 1993 to 1996 ten families built ten houses. It was a dream come true, even if it wasn't a plotland! Here he is doing his best to tile a roof.

However Shepperton-on-Thames where the author lived from 1959 to 1966 had hundreds of plotland houses which had gone un-noticed as he grew up there. His mum continued to live in Shepperton until recently so there were occasional opportunities to take photographs. This book is the result of that informal documentary activity between 2004 - 2016.

69. Three music Improvisation Rites for Shepperton

Stolen rite - Move your head like swaying leaves, then... drumming like gusts of wind. (See Worsley 1968 p.62)
Rite of change -The physical appearance of the players changes dramatically. (ibid p.70)
Rite of adaptation - Men adopt the custom of carrying a walking-sticks. Women wear paper boats as hats. The insect spirits can be heard whistling as they pass overhead. (ibid p.70)

Ingram Content Group UK Ltd.
Milton Keynes UK
UKHW051612240423
420694UK00002B/24